Praise for
Achieving Financial Fulfillment

"The mountain of information and competing ideologies on the internet has made it such a challenge to find objective answers to even the simplest of financial questions. So many people are stumbling around in the dark. What a refreshing consolidation of the most important financial topics every household should aim to understand."

— **Devon Klumb**, Betterment for Advisors

"What a fantastic resource for anyone looking to get their financial house in order! Achieving Financial Fulfillment *does a great job of balancing what you need to know without being overly technical. This book can help anyone build a strong foundation for their financial life."*

— **Roger Pine**, CEO and Co-Founder, Holistiplan

*"*Achieving Financial Fulfillment *does an excellent job of covering the important areas of financial planning simply and thoroughly. I especially like the way it informs readers just how important planning ahead and living within your means are to your financial wellness. Investors have a lot to consider when choosing a financial advisor, and Chapter 5 makes it clear that a Fiduciary and Fee-Only advisor puts the needs of the client first."*

— **Allan Slider**, Founder, Fee-Only Network

Achieving Financial Fulfillment

*Remove the Stress of Financial Decisions
to Live the Life You Imagine*

Michael Helveston, CFP®, CRPC®

To My Parents and My Sister,

who always showed me The Way,

and kept me on track.

To My Wonderful Wife,

my life partner through thick and thin,

who makes me laugh every day and let's me be myself.

and to My Children,

who have enriched our lives and inspire me

to be my best. I love you all!

Table of Contents

Introduction   9

Chapter 1
How Emotional Decisions Can Get You Off Track   13

Chapter 2
Live Within Your Means   23

Chapter 3
Investing Principles   29

Chapter 4
If you fail to plan, you are planning to fail!"   39

Chapter 5
What Is the Best Type of Financial Advice?   47

Chapter 6
Understanding the Impact of Taxes   53

Chapter 7
Protecting What You've Got   63

Chapter 8
Adjusting Your Plans over Time   69

Chapter 9
Passing on What You Have and What You Have Learned   75

Conclusion   83

Achieving Financial Fulfillment

ISBN 979-8-9896-0800-3

Copyright © 2024 by Michael Helveston. All rights reserved.

1st Edition, January 2024

Project Editor - Conni Francini, *www.reedsy.com*

Cover and Interior Design - Bruce DeRoos, *www.lcoast.com*

The material provided in this book is for informational purposes only and is not intended to be a source of advice with respect to the material presented. The information and/or documents contained in this book do not constitute legal or financial advice and should never be used without first consulting with a financial professional to determine what may be best for your individual needs.

The publisher and the author do not make any guarantee or other promise as to any results that may be obtained from using the content of this book. You should never make any investment decision without first consulting with your own financial advisor and conducting your own research and due diligence. To the maximum extent permitted by law, the publisher and the author disclaim any and all liability in the event any information, commentary, analysis, opinions, advice and/or recommendations contained in this book prove to be inaccurate, incomplete or unreliable, or result in any investment or other losses.

Introduction

When was the last time you heard a financial news headline and wondered if it was something you should be worried about? Last week? This morning on TV or on the way to work? The financial media does a great job of pumping out lots of information, but how do you sort through it all to determine what, if anything, you should do about it?

As human beings we are programmed to fail when it comes to many financial decisions and investing. After all, we are not taught how to manage our finances in school. We may rely on others who may appear to know what they are doing and end up 'following the herd' with no clear direction. It's also easy to get into debt if you have to have the latest 'toys' and 'gadgets' that others do in order to feel satisfied and accomplished. Sticking to your own priorities and living within your means is easier said than done without a budget framework (more on that in Chapter 2). The good news is that there is no one 'right' path to success, and it's normal for each of us to find our own way as our knowledge and experience grows.

Once you get established in your working career, more opportunities and financial decisions will come your way. You may consider investing in more aggressive or risky ways in order to grow your money, but you also need to be fully aware of the downside, including potential investment declines and negative tax implications. It's also important to plan ahead by thinking about your short-term and long-term goals. If you don't make a plan to get somewhere in life, how will you know what path to take or when you have arrived? Don't be afraid to ask for help along the way to keep you on the straight and narrow path. It's easy to get sidetracked, so it's best to set up automatic savings and investment strategies to make sure they happen on a regular basis.

Of course, you're not done with financial planning as you approach retirement either. Here you will be faced with big decisions such as when to take Social Security, how long to stay in your home and how to plan your legacy. In this phase you may even redefine your 'why' or purpose, and rethink what your savings and investments will be used for in the future. Are you looking forward to a lifestyle of travel and relaxation, spending time with family and friends or something else?

Based on more than two decades of counseling, advising, and most importantly listening to clients, this book is a collection of financial guidance designed to help you live a full and worry-free life. My hope is that your financial concerns can take a back seat in life, so you may be free to set your sights on how you really want to spend your time. After all, time is a precious and valuable commodity, so why spend it stressing about money?

My goal with each chapter that follows is to help you do the little things right, avoid big mistakes, and achieve financial fulfillment.

Chapter 1: *How Emotional Decisions Can Get You Off Track*, shares the foundation for good financial decision-making and why we need to recognize when our emotions are leading our decisions instead of using facts to guide us.

In **Chapter 2**: *Live Within Your Means*, we explore how to create a budget that you can live with and the importance of setting up an emergency fund.

Chapter 3: *Investing Principles* lays out the core building blocks of an investment portfolio and key economic factors such as inflation and market volatility.

Chapter 4: *"If you fail to plan, you are planning to fail!"* lays out a clear case for why you should consider investing early in your life and the powerful growth engine that we all have access to known as compound interest!

In **Chapter 5**: *What Is the Best Type of Financial Advice?*, we break down the different types of advice you can receive and the importance of working with a Fiduciary Advisor.

Chapter 6: *Understanding the Impact of Taxes*, details why investing is not just about how much you make but how much you get to keep after taxes that really matters.

In **Chapter 7**: *Protecting What You've Got,* we review the most common insurance coverages you should consider and ways to keep your premiums down.

Chapter 8: *Adjusting Your Plans over Time* explains what should be covered with a financial checkup as well as important age milestones on the path to retirement.

Chapter 9: *Passing on What You Have and What You Have Learned* outlines the essentials of a proper estate plan, charitable giving strategies, and ways to strategically share your good fortune with your family members.

Lastly, the ***Conclusion*** reviews key takeaways from the book and includes thoughts for the future.

CHAPTER 1

How Emotional Decisions Can Get You Off Track

How many decisions do you think the average person makes each day? According to a study by Psychology Today, the average adult makes an estimated 35,000 decisions every day! That may seem like a high number, but if you think about it, with every choice we make there are many factors to consider, which are decisions along the way. For example, did you choose to roll your eyes when you read the number 35,000, or did you keep reading to learn more? What choices or decisions did you make about breakfast today, such as whether to have cereal, eggs, or fruit? If you chose to eat cereal, which kind did you choose? Which size spoon did you choose? Did you choose to sit or stand to eat? Or, did you decide to eat in the car or simply skip breakfast altogether? Whew! The point is that we are constantly faced with many seemingly trivial decisions that are often linked to our emotions. These small choices can play a big factor in what we do and say. So, of the 35,000 decisions you will make today, how many of those do you think are financial decisions?

The purpose of this book is to help you make smart financial choices, instead of emotional choices. This starts with being aware of how we choose, how emotions impact our choices, and ultimately how emotional decisions can impact our financial lives. We want things to go according to plan. That is why we make plans in the first place, right?

When it comes to financial planning, the most common emotional mistakes occur in managing investments. These mistakes occur due to common emotional biases. Below are four of the most common biases (emotions) that can impact our thoughts and decisions:

Herding Bias

The practice of herding livestock has taken place for centuries. Some animals form herds on their own as a form of protection against predators and to move together to the most fertile grasslands. But is herding a good practice for investors? The fear of missing out (or FOMO) is a real human behavior. People follow the actions of others they believe have done their research but are followers themselves!

Real-Life Example

The tech or 'dot-com' bubble of the late 1990s was perhaps one of the best examples of an investment trend based on herding. People with little or no experience bought technology stocks that seemed to be continuously rising in price because other people said they were "making a ton of money." Many of those companies had no significant earnings record or sustainable profits and fell apart or went out of business once the economy eventually slowed down. The panicked buying created by FOMO was later followed by panicked selling. as people tried to preserve some of their remaining gains and limit losses. The tech-heavy Nasdaq market lost more than 75% of its value in 2000 and did not return to its prior peak value until 2015.

Familiarity Bias

Do you think that flipping houses is a risky proposition? You buy a property at what you think is a fair price, spend money on renovations and improvements, and hope you can sell it for more than what you put into it to make a profit. What do you think about someone who has successfully flipped twenty houses? Do you think that person feels the same level of risk? The risk each time is no different. Once you become familiar with something, the risks may seem to decline or be less concerning. Familiarity bias is our preference for situations, outcomes, and patterns that we have previously observed.

Real-Life Example

I was working with a client for a few years when she approached me about investing in a limited partnership that was buying properties in New York City. She explained that her brother had invested in similar strategies over many years with no issues while earning a high rate of return. She had grown comfortable with this type of investment over time due to her brother's positive experience and her many conversations about it with him. She said that she saw it as a "no-lose" situation based on the pattern of steady past returns.

Real estate limited partnerships are generally not liquid, as they require several years for the properties to be acquired and rented and may take time for the properties to be sold. Based on this I suggested she continue with a more liquid stock and bond portfolio that we had established. She chose instead to invest $40,000 in the limited partnership. Unfortunately, after only six months of receiving the promised income from the investment, the payments stopped. Within a few weeks she learned that the "investor" she had given her money to was charged with operating a Ponzi scheme. He had been taking money from new investors to pay interest to the prior investors. The investment illustrations and financial documentation she reviewed about the limited partnership before investing were fake.

The "investment" that was once believed to be very safe was in fact too good to be true. The silver lining for my client was that she had invested non-retirement money in the limited partnership. This entitled her to claim a partial tax loss on the investment, but in the end, this was still an extremely disappointing experience.

Confirmation Bias

I have been an avid Philadelphia sports fan for my whole life. For those of you who follow major sports leagues such as the NFL, NHL, MLB and NBA, you may pity me. For those of you who don't follow them, here is a brief synopsis: Our teams typically fall into the categories of *mediocre* and *competitive*, with only an occasional spectacular season. For example, The Philadelphia Eagles won Super Bowl LII in 2018. It was an unlikely yet spectacular victory over the highly favored New England Patriots. It was the first Super Bowl victory for the Eagles franchise, whose last NFL championship was in 1960, several years before the first Super Bowl in 1967. But was this championship a surprise to me? No. No? After a 58-year drought I saw this coming? Yes, and here's why.

I begin every football season with hope and optimism, starting with the NFL draft. At the draft our team is searching to find stars and leaders of the future. Their youth and enthusiasm fuels the excitement and promise for the new season ahead. In the weeks leading up to the season I can't stop reading posts and articles about how much the team has improved and how the new players that joined the team will make a difference. I steer clear of all the posts and articles about anything negative about the Eagles. I don't care to see their odds of winning the next Super Bowl (unless they are favored) or read about how good other teams could be this year. This is confirmation bias at its finest. I wear my favorite Eagles hat throughout the off season and keep an eye on potential player movements in hopes of my team landing a prized free agent. I even have a painting of the now famous "Philly Special" touchdown play from the Super Bowl in my office as a reminder that anything is possible.

When was the last time you did a Google search and scrolled past the first few results to find what you were looking for? If you haven't noticed yourself doing this before, you will now. It is a natural human tendency to seek information that we want to find in order to confirm our existing beliefs. Unfortunately, this type of bias can prevent us from looking at situations objectively. It can also influence the decisions we make and lead to poor or faulty choices.

Real-Life Example

Evaluating individual stocks is a good example of confirmation bias. You see a product or hear about a new company whose technology seems to make sense. In your mind this could be something that many people will need or appreciate, so you start to investigate it further. Now you start seeing a need for this product everywhere as you evaluate the prospects of the company's growth. Are you reading the articles that highlight the product's competitors? My guess is no. As Warren Buffet once said, "What the human being is best at doing is interpreting all new information so that their prior conclusions remain intact." You may also be more likely to trade investments more actively when your beliefs are confirmed by others because it leads to a sense of overconfidence. However, it may also cause you to expect higher returns on investments than what is justified. The bottom line is that we need to seek out facts to limit the impact of confirmation bias on our decisions.

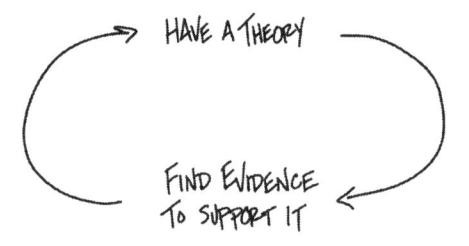

Recency Bias

How different was yesterday from today, in terms of how you see your future and what your concerns are? My guess is not much different. And how does that differ from how you saw your future just five years ago? We are most likely comfortable with where we are today, so it is easy to assume we will feel about the same tomorrow as we do today. Our minds get comfortable with the current state of things in order to feel like we are in control, even though things are changing every day. Recency bias occurs when people emphasize recent events rather than looking at events over time.

Real-Life Example

As mentioned earlier, the NASDAQ Stock Market crashed in 2000, and the 'dot-com' bubble burst, causing a recession in the process. The Federal Reserve responded to the poor economic conditions by cutting the Federal Funds interest rates several times all the way down to 1.00% after September 11, 2001. They didn't start raising them again until 2004. I was working in the Personal Financial Planning division at Vanguard at the time, and I strongly remember that almost every client I spoke to was convinced that interest rates had "nowhere else to go but up". And they did go up. As the market and economy started to recover in 2003, the Federal Reserve raised rates from 1.00% to over 5.00%.

see chart, next page

FED RATE MOVES
The Fed's target for the fed funds rate, a key overnight lending rate.

THE RATE STAYS AT 5.25%

SOURCE: FEDERAL RESERVE

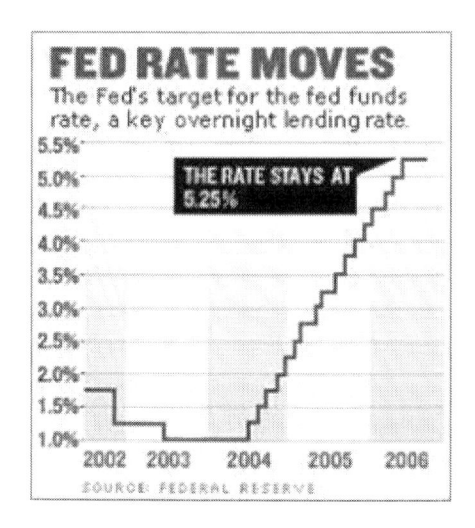

A short time later in 2007, the Fed began cutting rates again to help with the crumbling economy during the financial crisis that had begun. So, in 2003 no one could imagine that the Federal Reserve would reverse course on interest rates just a few years later. After all they had "nowhere else to go but up." This seemed like a logical expectation at the time. The Recency Bias had allowed most investors to become comfortable with the current trend, and it seemed illogical that the trend could reverse fairly quickly. Does this sound like the interest rate movements in 2022 and 2023?

Dalbar Study

There are other emotions that can impact your ability to make sound financial decisions including regret, overconfidence, and fear. The financial research firm DALBAR has compiled years of analysis on human behavior and its impact on investor returns. What they repeatedly have found is striking: on average people experience lower returns than the investments they are holding simply because they are influenced by emotions and buy and sell at the wrong times. In essence, as human beings we are not necessarily programmed to be good investors. We get excited and overconfident in our own decisions when things are going well and want to run and hide when markets fall.

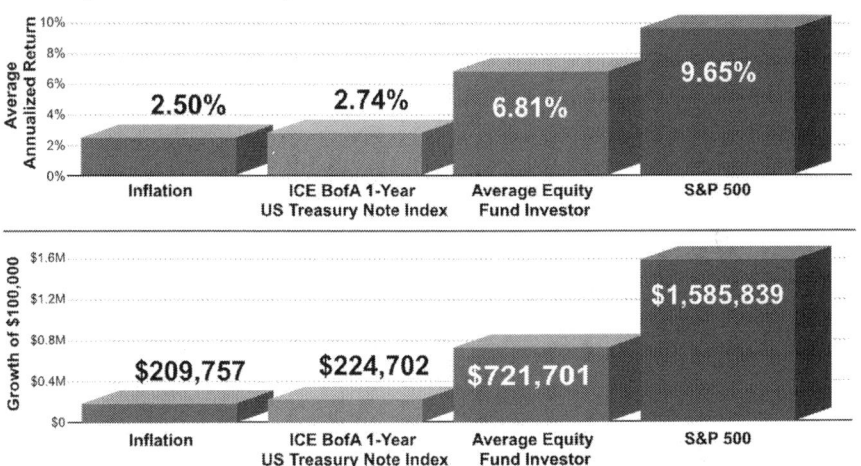

The Dalbar Study: Average Equity Fund Investor vs. Indexes Over 30 Years
30 Years (1/1/1993 - 12/31/2022)

	Inflation	ICE BofA 1-Year US Treasury Note Index	Average Equity Fund Investor	S&P 500
Average Annualized Return	2.50%	2.74%	6.81%	9.65%
Growth of $100,000	$209,757	$224,702	$721,701	$1,585,839

Average Equity Investor as determined by Dalbar | Study source: Dalbar QAIB 2023 study, Morningstar, Inc. | Past performance does not guarantee future results. The S&P 500 Index is an unmanaged float-adjusted market capitalization-weighted index that is generally considered representative of the U.S. stock market. Other indexes may be more appropriate to benchmark your investments against. It is not possible to invest directly in an index. Data is provided for illustrative purposes only, it does not represent actual performance of any client portfolio or account and it should not be interpreted as an indication of such performance. © 2023 Index Fund Advisors, Inc. (IFA.com)

My opinion may be biased, but this makes a pretty strong argument for seeking professional advice when it comes to navigating the world of personal finances and the many decisions involved. An independent and unbiased advisor should be less likely to be subject to the emotional ups and downs as you would be with your own money. We'll explore the different types of financial advice in detail later.

Simple Steps to Achieving Financial Fulfillment

What could you relate to in Chapter 1?

- Have you experienced FOMO or other biases? Did they get you off track?

- How can you respond to these biases differently in the future?

CHAPTER 2

Live Within Your Means

We all have to start somewhere. Our childhood and upbringing have a significant impact on who we become as individuals and how we view the world around us. What is your earliest memory? I can remember walking home from the grocery store at age 5 or 6 with my mom and practicing how to spell my middle name. I repeated S-c-o-t-t, S-c-o-t-t, S-c-o-t-t! I'm not sure how many other days I had spent practicing and repeating it back to my parents, but after a while I got it! What is your first memory involving money as a child? I'll never forget being in 5th grade and a teacher asking the class if anyone had a bank account. A few kids raised their hands, but I didn't because I didn't have one. I remember going home that day and declaring to my parents that I wanted one. It wasn't long before I got my first savings account, and my interest in finance started to really grow (along with the *interest* in my account).

Financial principles are no different from other behaviors: we learn them by watching others, practicing, and repeating. A common statement about money is to Live within your means.' What does that mean exactly? To me, that is simply making the most of what you have whether it is a little or a lot. If you spend everything that you make, you will have no savings. I have worked with many people who were able to save a large sum of money over time by being disciplined with their saving and investing. The "millionaire next door" is a real thing! So, no matter your income, some portion needs to be set aside for the unexpected and the future.

Whether you are just starting out or are later in your career, a good target is to save 10% of your income. You first need to establish a cushion for one-time expenses such as car maintenance, vacations, and unplanned costs such as medical bills. Once you have a basic emergency fund of a few hundred to a few thousand dollars, unplanned expenses will no longer feel like an emergency situation. This money can be kept in a checking, savings, or money market account for easy access.

Next, a common strategy is to divide your income into different categories based on how the money will be used. The percentages used for the categories can be customized, but the categories are typically the same: Needs, Wants, and Savings/Debt.

Here is a breakdown of how you can allocate your income:

        50% of your income: Needs

        30% of your income: Wants

        20% of your income: Savings/Debt

Needs

We all have necessary expenses. This portion of your budget should cover costs such as housing, food, transportation, utilities, insurance and minimum payments on loans. Anything beyond the minimum payment should go into the Savings/Debt repayment category.

Wants

Distinguishing between Needs and Wants isn't always easy and can vary from one budget to another. Generally, Wants are the extras that aren't essential to living and working costs. They're often just for fun and include meals out, entertainment, and travel.

Savings/Debt

Savings is the amount you put away to prepare for the future. You can start by creating a comfortable cash cushion to avoid taking on future debt. Further, you will need to devote your savings to paying down existing debt (including beyond the minimum payments). How to use this part of your budget depends on your situation, and it likely will include saving for retirement through accounts such as a 401(k), IRA or Roth IRA.

Real-Life Example

Suppose your take-home pay (after taxes) is $5,000 per month. Here is how that could be divided up:

Needs - 50% of $5,000 = $2,500

  $1,200 rent/housing

  $400 car payment/insurance

  $300 food

  $300 utilities/cell phone

  $200 minimum loan payments

  $100 miscellaneous

  $2,500 total

Wants - 30% of $5,000 = $1,500

  $600 entertainment/hobbies

  $400 meals out

  $300 travel (or savings for big vacation)

  $100 gym membership

  $100 miscellaneous

  $1,500 total

Savings/Debt -20% of $5,000 = $1,000

  $500 Roth IRA contribution

  $300 added to savings/checking account

  $200 extra loan payments

  $1,000 total

In this example, 10% of the take-home pay or $500/month is contributed to a Roth IRA. Setting aside even small amounts of money is critical no matter your stage in life. Out of sight is out of mind! You will thank yourself later when the savings start to really add up. Also, as your income increases, it can become more valuable to fund a pre-tax account such as a 401(k) in order to get a current year income tax deduction. You should always try to take advantage of company matching and benefits provided by your employer. The most important thing is to automate your savings every month (or every paycheck) so it happens without having to think about it.

The order for using your money in this category matters as well. The first priority is to build a cash reserve, and the second priority is to pay down debts. The third priority is investing. Some debts are better than others, such as a home mortgage or a car loan. However, I believe that investing should begin only after credit card debts are paid-off in full. Even a low interest rate on a credit card is likely to be the same or higher than the potential long-term returns associated with investing.

Any planning for where your money is allocated and how it is spent should also include ways to organize your finances. There are many apps and websites you can use to track your spending. In addition, keeping your financial records in order should reduce stress and may prevent future headaches when you need to get your hands on something quickly. You just need to decide what to keep, where to keep it, and when your files should be updated again.

Consider these six categories for organizing your finances:

1. Basic Finances – bank statements, credit card information, loan records

2. Investments – retirement accounts, stocks
3. Income Taxes – tax returns, paystubs
4. Insurance – original policies and recent statements
5. Estate Documents – wills, powers of attorney, trusts, living wills
6. Legal Documents – real estate transactions, birth/marriage/divorce records, passports

It's also important to communicate to a family member or friend what you have done and where things are located, so they can help if needed.

Simple Steps to Achieving Financial Fulfillment

What could you relate to in Chapter 2?

- Do you have a budget? If so, does it include a savings component and is it automated?

- What could you do to better organize your finances?

CHAPTER 3

Investing Principles

So, what is all the fuss about? Investing can sound wonderful if you hear a story of someone who has experienced tremendous investment returns or has accumulated millions of dollars in a short amount of time. Other times it might sound downright terrifying when you learn of someone who lost everything when their company went out of business or the market tanked.

The first thing I suggest is to determine whether you want to trade stocks or invest in stocks for the long-term toward a goal. I think many of us often confuse these two activities. Let's start by defining what I mean by the terms *trader* and *investor*. Trading is the buying and selling of individual securities with the hope of making a short-term profit. Investing involves the purchase of diversified investments and holding them for a long period of time.

Most of us would probably classify ourselves as investors by these definitions. Yet when we think of investing, we are more likely to act like traders. Why is that? Consider what you see and hear in the news. The financial media is full of headlines that are designed to catch your eye and your emotions. Article titles such as, "The Top 10 Stocks You Should Own Now" or "Five Things You Need to Know…", appear often. These kinds of lists grab your attention because they share ideas that appear to be urgent. And don't we all want to do the best we can with our investments? We are not only influenced by the financial media. When your best friend tells you about a stock or mutual fund she bought that's sure to keep making money, doesn't your brain tell you that you should do something, like consider buying it? This reactionary thinking may not lead to sound decision making.

If you are reading this book, you probably see yourself as an investor. So what can you do to be a better one? How can you fight the urge to act like a trader whenever the market becomes volatile?

First of all, don't overreact. For example, let's say you look at your 401(k) statement and see that, of your six funds, three are losing money while three other funds are up significantly. Do you feel compelled to take the money from the underperforming funds and move it into the funds that are doing well? Unfortunately, this is often done without thought to the overall asset allocation, diversification, and the risk level of each investment. This short-term thinking can cause you to buy into funds that are at the top of their cycle and sell out of funds at the bottom. Does buying high and selling low sound like a strategy you should employ?

Also, know that you are not alone, and market volatility can be difficult for anyone to handle. You'll notice in the chart below that both stocks and bonds can experience very high and very low returns in any single year. However, as you move into 5-, 10-, and 20-year investing periods, the range of cumulative returns is reduced greatly, and in every rolling 20-year period since 1950, stocks and bonds always ended up with positive results. Lastly, remember the Dalbar Study we looked at earlier showed that it's best to maintain a long-term focus because your emotions may drive you to get in and out of the market, leading to underperforming the average returns of the market over time.

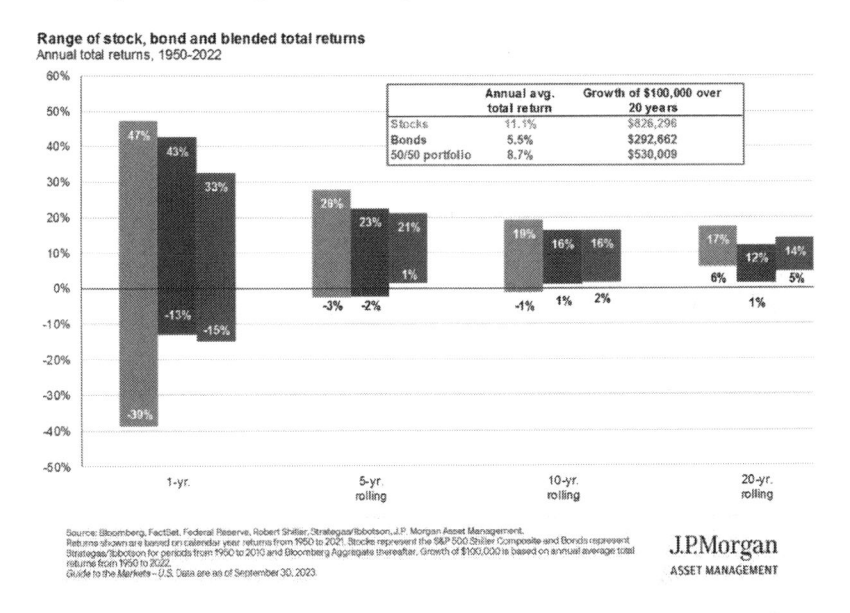

Range of stock, bond and blended total returns
Annual total returns, 1950-2022

	Annual avg. total return	Growth of $100,000 over 20 years
Stocks	11.1%	$826,296
Bonds	5.5%	$292,662
50/50 portfolio	8.7%	$530,009

Source: Bloomberg, FactSet, Federal Reserve, Robert Shiller, Strategas/Ibbotson, J.P. Morgan Asset Management.
Returns shown are based on calendar year returns from 1950 to 2021. Stocks represent the S&P 500 Shiller Composite and Bonds represent Strategas/Ibbotson for periods from 1950 to 2010 and Bloomberg Aggregate thereafter. Growth of $100,000 is based on annual average total returns from 1950 to 2022.
Guide to the Markets – U.S. Data are as of September 30, 2023.

J.P.Morgan
ASSET MANAGEMENT

Before going any further, let's take a step back and understand some of the standard investment terminology and how they are related. There are many investment vehicles that are beyond the scope of this book. These include limited partnerships, annuities, and real estate investment trusts, as well as sub-categories of stocks such as large, small, international, growth, value, corporate, municipal, etc. This book focuses on the fundamentals.

Stocks

Over my career in the financial advisory industry I have developed what I hope are simple ways to explain complex topics. When it comes to investing, I advise clients to focus on companies. In any given year there are many distractions, from the current state of the economy to geopolitical events to gas prices. All of that other data is either a head-wind or tail-wind for companies. For example, will the upcoming election impact how many 2-liter bottles of Coca-Cola will sell next year? It might, but odds are good it might not. Companies, unlike commodities such as gold or oil, are run by a management team (no matter how big or small) that are trying to deliver profits to their shareholders. So, investing over time is about going along for the ride as companies navigate the current economic environment and adjust to ever-changing conditions. Not all companies survive forever, so diversification is extremely important!

Stocks give you partial ownership in a corporation, while bonds are a loan from you to a company. In general, a stock investor hopes to have the stock price of the company appreciate in value and be sold later for a gain. Most bond investments are made to earn a fixed amount of interest over time.

When you buy stock, you're actually purchasing a tiny piece of the company, called shares. For example, if the price of a stock is $25 per share and you invest $10,000, you will end up owning 400 shares ($10,000 / $25 each). As a partial owner you will share in the company's successes (and failures), so if the stock price rises over time to $50 per share, your investment would have grown to $20,000 (400 x $50 each). You could sell those shares and realize a gain of $10,000, or you can keep holding them into the future.

Bonds

When you buy a bond (similar to buying a bank certificate of deposit), you are purchasing a security that is designed to pay you interest over time for a set period, after which it will pay back the full amount you bought the bond for, called the maturity date. Bonds may sound relatively safe but aren't completely risk-free. If the company goes bankrupt during the bond holding period, you may stop receiving interest payments or may not get back your full principal.

Real-Life Example

To illustrate how the interest on a bond works, let's say you buy a bond for $25,000, and it pays 2% annual interest for 10 years. That means every year you would receive $500 in interest payments (2% x $25,000). After 10 years you would have earned $5,000 in interest and then get back your initial investment of $25,000.

Cash

As we reviewed earlier, the money you keep in your bank checking or savings account is not intended for investment; instead it is set aside for easy access and potential future expenses. Most brokerage investment accounts also include a cash position that is used to purchase investments, and this is also the place where cash from the proceeds of an investment sale are received and held. Certificates of deposit (CDs), treasury bills, money market mutual funds and high-yield savings accounts are also considered low-risk investments. Some of these may be covered by the Federal Deposit Insurance Corporation (FDIC).

Mutual Funds

Mutual funds are collections of stocks, bonds, or other securities that might be difficult to put together on your own. These collections are called portfolios. The price of the mutual fund is determined by the total value of the securities in the portfolio, divided by the number of the fund's outstanding shares. This price, called a Net Asset Value (NAV), fluctuates based on the value of the securities held by the portfolio at the end of each business day. Mutual fund investors only own shares in the fund itself and don't actually own the securities inside the fund.

ETFs

Exchange-traded funds (ETFs) combine both the aspects of mutual funds and those of individual stocks. Like a mutual fund, an ETF is a pooled investment fund in a diversified portfolio of investments. But unlike mutual funds, ETF shares trade like stocks on an exchange and can be bought or sold throughout the day. In addition to low fees, most ETFs have low turnover (buying and selling within the fund), which helps to keep down the amount of capital gains realized and passed on to the individual investor. This may be a way to reduce or minimize your income tax burden.

Historically, most mutual funds were actively managed by professionals, with fund managers buying and selling securities within the fund in an attempt to beat the market and help investors profit. However, passively managed index funds have become increasingly popular in recent years.

Ironically, while ETFs were historically passively managed (as they typically tracked a broad market index or sub-sector), there are a growing number of actively-managed ETFs. As they have already shown, the types and styles of investment vehicles will continue to evolve over time.

Standard Deviation (volatility)

Understanding this measurement can provide useful insights when choosing investment options, as not all returns are created equal. Standard deviation is a common statistical measurement of volatility that tells you how far apart all of the values are from the average (or mean) value. Two investments can have the same average return over time but may have taken very different paths to get there.

Real-Life Example

If Mutual Fund A has an average annual return of 10% and a standard deviation of 4%, you would expect about 68% of the time (see chart below) for the return to be between 6% (10% - 4%) and 14% (10% + 4%), which is one standard deviation on either side of 10%. About 95% of the time you would expect the return to be between 2% (10% - 8% (now 2 * 4%) and 18% (10% + 8%), or two standard deviations on either side of 10%. This assumes the fund's returns follow a normal distribution or what is commonly called a bell curve. In a normal distribution, 68% of values are within one standard deviation of the mean, 95% of values are within two standard deviations of the mean, and 99.7% of values are within three standard deviations of the mean.

see chart next page

68% of values are within
1 standard deviation of the mean

95% of values are within
2 standard deviations of the mean

99.7% of values are within
3 standard deviations of the mean

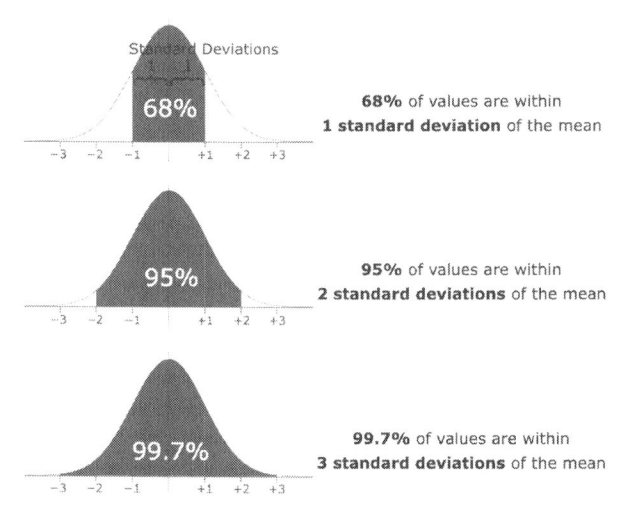

Pierce, Rod. (1 Feb 2022). "Normal Distribution". Math Is Fun. Retrieved 23 Oct 2023 from http://www.mathsisfun.com/data/standard-normal-distribution.html

If Mutual Fund B has an average annual return of 10% and a standard deviation of 15%, you would expect about 68% of the time for the return to be between -5% (10% - 15%) and 25% (10% + 15%). About 95% of the time you would expect the return to be between -20% (10% - 30% (now 2* 15%) and 40% (10% + 30%).

As you can see, not all returns are created equal! The volatility would be much greater with Mutual Fund B, even though they have the same average return. In my opinion, dealing with volatility often causes people to make decisions that may not be in their best interest. If you don't think you would react well with a fund that has wild swings, perhaps you should consider one with a lower standard deviation.

Inflation

When I was a young child, I remember driving past the local gas station and seeing that a gallon of regular cost $0.86 (in 1979).

Jimmy Carter was the President of the United States, a first-class stamp cost $0.15, and the Dow Jones Industrial Average hit a high of 907 that year.

907? Really, is that all? The same Dow Jones that as of this writing has been as high as 36,000? Maybe this was just a really great period of time to invest. Maybe there were no significant world events to cause a setback...or were there? What about President Reagan being shot, the 1987 Stock Market Crash, September 11th, the Lehman Brothers bankruptcy in 2008, or the COVID-19 pandemic?

The point is that costs will continue to rise over time, and investing in stocks, as evidenced by the Dow Jones, would have allowed you to keep ahead of inflation and grow your money in spite of all the negative world events. Stock investments tend to increase over time because of great companies and their management teams. The best companies plan for the future and then adjust based on the circumstances.

Simple Steps to Achieving Financial Fulfillment

What could you relate to in Chapter 3?

- Did you associate long-term investing with at least a 5-year period?
- Have you ever second-guessed your investment strategy when the market went down?
- How do you think you could respond differently in the future?

CHAPTER 4

"If you fail to plan, you are planning to fail!"

— *Benjamin Franklin*

This quote by Benjamin Franklin can apply to many choices—especially those about personal finances. If we don't take his message to heart, then a lack of planning can be costly. For example, look at the illustration below to see just how important it is to start saving and investing early. Starting just 10 years earlier at age 25 instead of 35, the projected investment balance for Jack at age 65 is more than double that of Jill! Joey is even farther behind by waiting until age 45 to start saving for retirement.

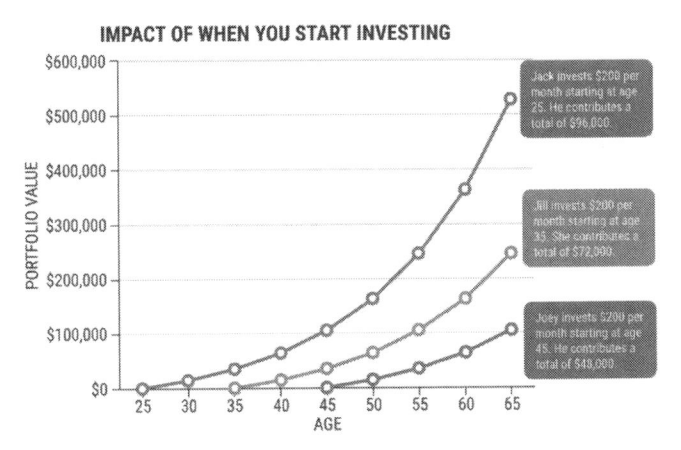

IMPACT OF WHEN YOU START INVESTING

Jack invests $200 per month starting at age 25. He contributes a total of $96,000.

Jill invests $200 per month starting at age 35. She contributes a total of $72,000.

Joey invests $200 per month starting at age 45. He contributes a total of $48,000.

Hicks, Coryanne and Hellman, Nate. (3 Aug 2023). "Impact of When You Start Investing". US News Money. Retrieved 23 Oct 2023 from *https://money.usnews.com/investing/investing-101/articles/2018-07-23/9-charts-showing-why-you-should-invest-today*, assumes 7% growth per year.

An extremely important principle at work in the chart is compound interest. If you take nothing else away from reading this book remember this: it's possible for your money to make more money for you with no additional effort!

> Let's look at how saving early can make a difference: If you invest $10,000 and earn 5% interest in the first year, you would have made $500 ($10,000 * 0.05) in interest and have a total of $10,500. In the next year, you start with $10,500 invested at the same 5% interest, and it now earns you $525 ($10,500 x 0.05) in interest. So, your $500 earned in the first year made you an additional $25 ($500 x 0.05) of interest in the second year without any additional contribution from you, and so on and so on over time. This is how little numbers can become much bigger!

Also, setting up an automatic savings or investment plan is critical. No matter how small you start, you won't miss it if it's out of sight, out of mind. For example, you could have a certain dollar amount from each paycheck go into a savings account. Further, you could put a fixed percentage of your salary into a retirement account, such as a 401(k), in order to make sure you save on a regular basis and learn to live on what is left over.

As you can see, financial planning is a process to help you achieve your goals over time, not just a once- and-done event. It is also about much more than managing investments to get the highest return. Investments are a key component, but there are many other items that should be considered.

Set Realistic Goals

The first step is to set realistic goals for where you want to be in the future. If you prefer, you can work with an advisor who can help you to get organized. A written statement of your goals or a detailed plan can be developed to create a point of reference. Saving for retirement may be your most important long-term goal: you'll likely have other financial goals, too. Maybe you would like to save for a vacation, pay down your debts, or buy a house in the near future.

Assess Your Investment Options

The second step is to assess your investment options. Investing that involves the use of stocks should only be considered when the time frame is long-term, generally five years or more. This is due to volatility and short-term declines that should be anticipated because of the many factors that could impact the value of a business. These can include changes in the company leadership, competition in the industry, or outside influences, such as geopolitical events or changes in the overall economy.

Determine Your Asset Allocation

The third and final step once your time horizon is understood, is to determine the asset allocation (or mix of stocks, bonds, etc.) to be used to achieve the goal. This is determined by taking into account the desired financial outcome and your risk tolerance (how much risk/reward potential is acceptable). Other factors to consider include how much money to set aside, your current sources of income, other investment and/or retirement accounts available, and the potential income tax implications of investing.

There are many choices when it comes to investment strategies. A simple way to group them is to identify them as aggressive, moderate, or conservative. Most investment companies have their own definition of what fits into these groups. Determining the rate of return that will be needed or what you assumed in your projections is an important part of planning how you will reach your goals. From this information, an initial asset allocation can be determined.

- Aggressive allocations are typically assumed to have the highest return potential and also the greatest short-term volatility. For example, portfolios with 70% - 100% in stocks (and the balance in bonds or cash) may be considered aggressive.

- Conservative portfolios are typically for more risk-averse investors and are expected to have less volatility and potentially lower returns. 0% - 30% in stocks may be considered conservative.

- Moderate allocations cover everything in between. 30% - 70% stocks may be considered moderate.

The asset allocation should be revisited over time to determine whether your investment strategy should change and to monitor progress towards your goals.

The asset allocation between stocks, bonds and cash is said to be the single greatest factor in influencing portfolio returns. That means that the specific stock, mutual fund or ETF you buy is less important than you may think. Obviously, finding the next great company and buying it when the price is low would be nice as well, but that is much less likely and you should focus on what you can control. That is 1) what level of risk you are willing to assume and 2) diversifying in a way that allows you to capture the returns of the market over time and 3) reacting appropriately to what happens next (or in many cases not reacting at all!).

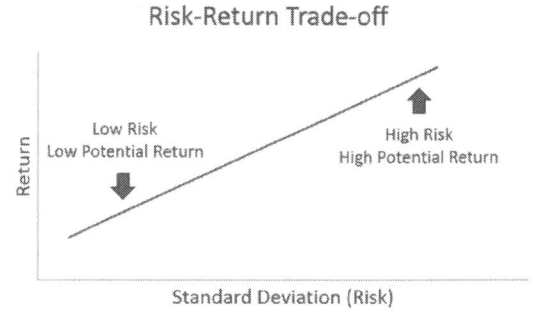

Risk-Return Trade-off

*Low Risk
Low Potential Return*

*High Risk
High Potential Return*

Return

Standard Deviation (Risk)

MI Research Team. (19 Sept 2018). "The Risk-Return Trade-Off". Model Investing. Retrieved 23 Oct 2023 from *https://modelinvesting.com/articles/the-risk-return-trade-off/*

I stated earlier that achieving financial fulfillment involved doing the little things right and avoiding big mistakes. In my experience, learning to expect short-term market volatility and to appreciate it as a possible opportunity is probably the single greatest factor in your success or failure in reaching your goals. Remember the DALBAR study: on average people experienced lower returns than the investments they were holding! This was simply because they were influenced by emotions and bought and sold at the wrong times.

Investing with a target asset allocation in place works because it does not rely on you needing to jump in and out of the best performing categories. It allows you to stay focused on your long-term goals. The inevitable volatility in the market then creates opportunities to rebalance your portfolio. You could end up over your target amount in bonds when the stock market goes down. If you are managing your money to stick with your initial asset allocation, this would prompt you to sell bonds and buy stocks while prices are lower (discounted from their recent highs). Of course, income tax implications of rebalancing should also be considered for assets held in taxable non-retirement accounts. This is maintaining your asset allocation from a *macro* view.

Asset allocation from a *micro* view looks at the different investment categories that make up the stock portion and the bond portion. For example, a typical portfolio could be made up of large, medium, and small U.S. companies, as well as international companies. Your bonds could be broken down into corporate, municipal, or government-issued securities.

Remember the 'dot-com' bubble when people were buying technology stocks like a 'herd,' only to see the Nasdaq market lose more than 75% of its value in 2000? A buy-and-hold strategy may not be as exciting as trying to find the next hot stock or using your intuition to try to time the market. However, it has shown to be a reliable approach for taking some of the emotion out of investing, so you can spend your time worrying about something else.

Another important part of financial planning is simplifying the management of your accounts whenever possible. If you have ever shopped around for the best bank CD rate, you may have found yourself opening a new one each year at a different bank. Or perhaps you found a great new job and left your 401(k) with your old employer. Maybe you started a new IRA with a different financial firm recently and have an old IRA you haven't touched in years.

No matter how you got them, you may find yourself with a collection of IRAs or accounts scattered around. What's worse is that they probably have no overall strategy and are not connected to each other. Did you know you will reach a point in retirement when you have to take money from each of your retirement accounts? There is a way to simplify that process and cut down on the recordkeeping by consolidating into a single account for each type you own. This includes that old 401(k), which you can probably rollover to an IRA with a brief phone call to the investment provider or by completing a form.

The benefits of consolidating your accounts include the following:

- **Less recordkeeping.** You will get fewer monthly statements, fewer emails and not as many forms at tax time.
- **Coordinated investments.** Ensuring a well-diversified portfolio can't be done easily with accounts spread out all over the place.
- **Simpler estate administration.** If you have ever settled someone's estate, you know all about this. More accounts mean more work and more complexity. Make it easy on your kids and/or your executor.
- **Easy required minimum distributions** (RMDs). At age 73 when RMDs start you don't want to have multiple IRA calculations each year. If the IRAs are consolidated, it's just one calculation! Also, if you need to figure out something like how much income tax to withhold, the calculation is simpler if it is based on just one account.

Simple Steps to Achieving Financial Fulfillment

What could you relate to in Chapter 4?

- Compound interest is a powerful concept. How can you make it work for you?

- Is your current asset allocation aggressive, moderate, or conservative?

- How can you simplify your financial recordkeeping?

CHAPTER 5

What Is the Best Type of Financial Advice?

The landscape for delivering and receiving financial advice is ever changing; however, investors typically fall into one of three categories: Do-It-Yourself (DIY), Limited Advice, and Full-Service Advice. Getting outside input on your situation is another way to remove anxiety about investing.

Do-It-Yourself

The internet and social media have opened the doors to making almost any task a potential do-it-yourself one. If you enjoy learning new information, researching a topic for yourself, or want more control over your decisions, you are probably a 'DIYer.' However, just like researching a medical term or diagnosis, trying to learn everything there is to know about a financial topic in five minutes may not be enough time. Fortunately, there are lots of tools available, such as Morningstar, which provides data on individual stocks, mutual funds, exchange-traded funds (ETFs), and more. Charles Schwab, E*TRADE, and Fidelity are examples of online brokers with low fees and minimums to get started that offer ample research as well.

Limited Advice

Let's say you want someone to manage your portfolio and want to be able to ask questions as they arise. In this case a robo-advisor, such as Betterment or Vanguard may be helpful. Typically, these services charge a lower fee (maybe 0.25% or more) to manage an investment portfolio based on your goals and use computer algorithms to maintain the strategy. Many of these financial institutions also offer the assistance of a company representative to provide limited additional guidance. Advisors that charge by the hour, on a project-based fee, or for an annual retainer with scheduled check-ins are also in this category. You may want help to do something straightforward without paying an ongoing fee for advice, such as set up college savings accounts or roll over an old 401(k) account. In this case you might want to start with XY Planning Network or NAPFA, where fee-for-service is a standard model for delivering advice. For example, you may be able to pay by the hour for a consultation, get ongoing advice with a monthly subscription plan, or have some of your account professionally managed for an annual fee.

Full-Service Advice

If you want to delegate the responsibility of managing your investments and overall finances, there are many full-service advisors. These advisory firms may bundle financial planning advice and money management as a combined service, so understanding their services and costs is important. Fees for ongoing advice usually average about 1% of the assets under management (AUM). In this service level you may receive tax and estate planning advice in addition to money management. In the AUM structure, you pay a percentage based on the amount of assets managed for you. If the fee is 1% of assets under management, and $500,000 of your money is managed, then you would pay a fee of $5,000 a year.

If you choose to pay for advice, understanding how advisors are compensated is critical. Many advisers try to eliminate conflicts of interest and act as fiduciaries by putting their client's needs ahead of their own. According to The Free Dictionary, the word *fiduciary* is from the Latin word *fiducia*, meaning "trust," and is a person who has the power and obligation to act for another under circumstances that require total trust, good faith, and honesty. The good news is that the industry has been evolving towards a future with continued emphasis on putting the client first. John Bogle, founder of Vanguard once said, "The ultimate good is serving the consumer" and that "I would call it being on the right side of history."[9]

According to The National Association of Personal Financial Advisors (NAPFA), there are three primary advisor compensation models:

Fee-Only Compensation

This model minimizes conflicts of interest. It is the required form of compensation for members of NAPFA. A Fee-Only financial advisor charges the client directly for his or her advice and/or ongoing management. No other financial reward is provided by any institution, which means that the advisor does not receive commissions on the actions they take on the clients' behalf. Compensation is based on an hourly rate, a percent of assets managed, a flat fee, or a retainer.

Fee-Based Compensation (fee and commission)

This form is often confused with Fee-Only, but it's not the same. Fee-based advisors charge clients a fee for the advice delivered, and they also sometimes receive payments for products they sell or recommend. In some cases, commissions are credited towards the fee, giving the appearance of a lower-priced option, but any outside compensation lessens the advisor's ability to keep the client's best interests first and foremost.

Commissions

Stockbrokers were initially needed to gain access to the market to buy and sell securities and charged a fee, called a commission, for each trade. NAPFA has always maintained that an advisor who is compensated through commissions is primarily a salesperson. A client working with a commissioned salesperson must always ask: Is this advice truly in my best interest, or is it the most profitable product for the advisor? Unfortunately, often the answer is the latter. In fact, a commissioned advisor could be putting the best interests of his employer ahead of the best interests of his client.

As you can see, it is essential to understand how your advisor is compensated for the advice you receive and whether they face hidden conflicts of interest. Make sure you understand and ask questions of any advisor about how their fees are structured and what services you will receive.

Simple Steps to Achieving Financial Fulfillment

What could you relate to in Chapter 5?

- Are you a DIYer or have you sought the advice of an Advisor?

- Which type of compensation model best suits you?

- What questions would you ask of an Advisor in the future?

CHAPTER 6

Understanding the Impact of Taxes

Again, it seems appropriate to quote Benjamin Franklin for his wisdom and understanding way back in 1789. "Our new Constitution is now established, everything seems to promise it will be durable; but, in this world, nothing is certain except death and taxes," Franklin said. Taxes continue to this day to be a certainty of life, so you'd better learn how best to live *with* them!

Any amount or method of saving money for retirement will help, right? Well, you are on the right track if you are delaying gratification by saving money for the future. Also, many people focus on trying to select investments that will produce the greatest returns over time, which makes sense, of course. However, as mentioned earlier, the asset allocation you choose (the mix of aggressive and/or conservative investments) will likely have the greatest impact on your results. So, if the specific investments you chose won't have as large of an impact as you might expect, what else might? The answer lies in trying to maximize your after-tax returns. Would you rather have a 10% return that is reduced to 7% after taxes or an 8% tax-free return? I think the answer is obvious.

There is a simple way to invest more efficiently and make the most of your contributions. It's called *asset location*, which is no more than paying attention to which account you use to buy certain types of securities. Over time, this can be a great way to maximize your after-tax returns without taking on any additional risk.

There are three major types of investment accounts, and they all have different tax treatment.

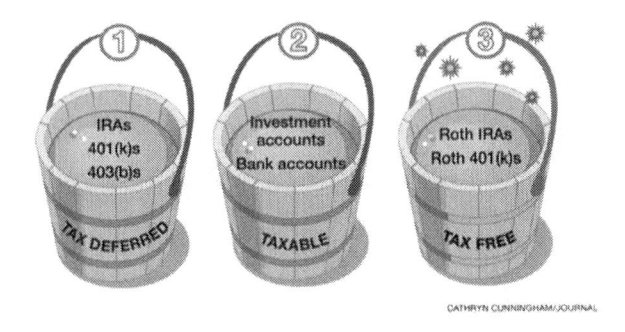

Cunningham, Cathryn. (4 Jan 2021). "Start the New Year with a Look at the Roth IRA". Albuquerque Journal. Retrieved 23 Oct 2023 from *https://www.abqjournal.com/business/start-the-new-year-with-a-look-at-the-roth-ira/article_2ca7b3ad-2c2a-5d01-8aaf-3da67269beae.html*

Tax-Deferred Accounts

As the name implies, typically the tax on these accounts is deferred until later when withdrawals are made. IRAs, 401(k)s, 403(b)s, and most company retirement accounts fall into this category. In most cases an income tax deduction is allowed for the year of the contribution, and there are annual limits as to how much can be added to these accounts.

Taxable Accounts

These are non-retirement investment accounts where what you earn is generally taxable each year. Common strategies for minimizing income taxes include passive investments, such as index funds or ETFs, and municipal bonds whose income is typically tax-exempt. Taxable accounts can be opened as a brokerage account, held directly with a mutual fund company, or as a transfer agent for buying individual stocks. A brokerage account is the most flexible, as it allows you to buy and sell a wide range of investment products.

Tax-Free Accounts

Your investment growth in these accounts, Roth IRAs and Roth 401(k)s, is generally tax-free over the years and also when withdrawn. There is no income tax deduction allowed in the year of the contribution, and there are annual limits on how much can be added to these accounts. You can also convert some tax-deferred accounts into Roth accounts, which includes paying the tax in the year of the conversion. This could make sense if you are in a low tax bracket now and expect to be in a higher one in retirement when the funds are used.

It is very common for people to simply save money in their company's tax-deferred savings plan and spend everything else, thinking they have done enough. The problem with this approach manifests itself at retirement. Every dollar distributed from a tax-deferred account is usually taxable. If you instead have money saved in a taxable account or a Roth IRA, you should have more flexibility and may have better control over how much tax you will pay on withdrawals by choosing which account is best.

Remember that we are taxed on interest and dividends. These two items are usually taxed as ordinary income, meaning they are taxed at the highest rates. Examples include CDs, taxable bond funds, and REITs, which you should try to purchase in a tax-deferred account, such as an IRA. It's best to hold stocks and stock mutual funds in an after-tax account, if possible. This is because long-term capital gains (held longer than 1 year) and qualified dividends are taxed at 15% for most taxpayers and 20% for those in the highest tax bracket. Ordinary income, though, can be as high as 39.6% plus an additional 3.8% surtax for some taxpayers. Also, stocks tend to be the most volatile, and if you experience a loss and sell, you can generally use the loss to offset gains in other positions. Municipal bonds also fit into this category.

IRAs and other tax-deferred accounts are a good place to buy taxable bonds, CDs, and high-turnover stock funds. If you enjoy trading stocks, an IRA might be a good place for this because there is no concern for short-term capital gains. In an after-tax account, these same short-term gains would be taxed as ordinary income.

Finally, we get to the Roth: the goose that lays golden eggs. There is something special about the phrase tax-free that makes me smile. If you think about it, $100,000 saved in a Roth IRA is worth $100,000, but $100,000 saved in a traditional IRA is only worth $70,000 if your combined tax rate upon withdrawal is 30%. Growth investments can be suitable in a Roth, with the goal of maximizing the tax-free growth and compounding over time.

There are other variables in asset location, and being aware of where you put your money greatly impacts how much you keep and what you receive when you take it out.

Here are a few other common tax-saving strategies:

1. **Long-term capital gains** – Hold investments a year or longer and gains are given favorable tax treatment over short-term gains (held less than 1 year), which are taxed as ordinary income.

2. **Qualified dividends** – Many investors like to hold dividend paying stocks or mutual funds. Pay close attention to the type of income your investment generates. Qualified dividends are taxed at a lower rate than ordinary dividends. For example, many REITs and partnerships pay ordinary dividends, which are taxed at your marginal (highest) tax bracket.

3. **Municipal bonds** – Over the years I have seen money managers invest in bonds that pay taxable interest without any regard for taxes, when there may be tax-free alternatives.

4. **Index funds and/or exchange traded funds (ETFs)** – Many index funds and ETFs have low turnover and as a result don't typically pass on as many capital gains distributions to shareholders as traditional mutual funds.

5. **Look Ahead at Your Income for Tax Bracket Changes** – Low income years may be good for intentionally taking on more income. (Would you pay 12% now to avoid a 22% tax later?) High-income years should be planned around by taking losses or deductions or deferring income to other years.

Let's look at an example of Roth IRA conversions that shows the importance of planning ahead and understanding the impact of taxes, specifically to consider converting IRA assets to a Roth IRA before drawing Social Security. Back in 2010, Roth IRA conversions became available to everyone because limits based on income and filing status were lifted. A conversion is typically a shift of pre-tax IRA (or 401(k)) money to a Roth IRA (or Roth 401(k)). The main benefit of a Roth conversion is that the money grows tax-free once inside the Roth IRA. The cost of the conversion is that the amount moved is taxed in the current year as income. It will take time to recover from the initial tax bill, but the savings over time can be substantial.

Real-Life Example

Let's say you retire at 58, and your new taxable income is $49,450 from pensions, investment earnings, and/or part-time work. You could convert $40,000 from a traditional IRA to a Roth IRA and stay within the 12% tax bracket (up to $89,450 ($49,450 + $40,000) of taxable income in 2023 for Married Filing Jointly). If you take advantage of this over the next four years you can convert a total of $160,000 ($40,000 x 4) into a Roth IRA. You have to pay taxes on the conversions, but remember that you would eventually pay tax on this money at RMD (Required Minimum Distribution) age AND anything it earns if left in your traditional IRA.

Here's the savings: the $160,000 now in the Roth IRA would earn about $450,000 over 20 years if invested at 7%. Not having to pay taxes on the $450,000 of growth at 12% tax saves you $54,000 ($450,000 x 12%)! This could be even more savings if your tax rate is higher in the future.

So why did we stop after 4 years? If you plan to draw Social Security at 62, the additional income from the Roth IRA conversion may cause your Social Security benefits to become taxable, thus reducing the savings of conversion. Currently, no one pays Federal income tax on more than 85% of his or her Social Security benefits. For example, if you file a joint return, and your combined income is between $32,000 and $44,000, you may have to pay income tax on up to 50% of your benefits. If more than $44,000, up to 85% of your benefits may be taxable.

Once again, you may be able to move a substantial portion of your IRA to a Roth IRA. As a great side benefit, lowering your IRA balance could lower your future RMDs. This could mean less tax on Social Security income in the future and less total taxes paid. As you can see it is important to be aware of this window of opportunity and all the specifics in order to take full advantage. Remember, saving money on taxes has the effect of compounding, giving you more to invest!

College Savings Accounts

529 Plans are tax-deferred college accounts where withdrawals for college and up to $10,000 per year in tuition for K-12 schools and up to $10,000 in student loan repayments are generally tax-free. The two major types allow you to either purchase college 'credits' at today's rates or to place your money in an investment account using mutual funds. A nice feature is that the beneficiary can usually be changed, if necessary, perhaps to another child. The owner is the parent or custodian who set up the account.

The downside with a 529 plan is that there is a 10% penalty on investment earnings upon withdrawal if the money is not used for qualified college expenses.

Another option that has been around even longer is the UGMA or Uniform Gift to Minors Account. As the name implies, contributions to these are a completed gift to the child but are controlled by the custodian until the child reaches the age of majority (typically 18 - 21 depending on the state). The funds in the account can be used for any purpose that benefits the child without penalty. However, they are considered an asset of the child for federal financial aid eligibility.

Roth IRAs are retirement accounts either in the parent's or child's name, and earned income from a job is required by either one or both to fund such accounts. There are also income limits that may restrict the use of Roth IRAs. Perhaps the greatest benefit of Roth IRAs is that contributions can be withdrawn at any time for any reason with no tax implications. Investment earnings are generally required to stay in a Roth IRA for 5 years and until age 59 ½. A plus is that these accounts are generally not considered part of the expected family contribution of either the parent or child for financial aid purposes.

These are just the major ways to save for college and the different tax treatment of the accounts. You can also use traditional savings accounts, brokerage accounts, and even U.S. Government Savings Bonds.

More on Capital Gains

The final area for a potential emotional mistake regarding taxes applies to capital gains. It's critical to not get stuck in certain investments because you are afraid of paying capital gains tax on the appreciation. With the stock market generally rising over time, there are typically only limited times where non-retirement investors realize losses. If you sell a mutual fund at a loss from your original purchase amount, you can apply up to $3,000 of the loss against your other income (after netting with any gains), and the rest of the loss can be carried over into future tax years at the federal tax level. Once the losses are used up, future capital gains would be subject to tax.

So, should you hold an appreciated asset to avoid paying capital gains tax? First, if you are charitably inclined, you could consider gifting appreciated assets. Typically, this approach enables you and the charity to avoid taxes. Qualified charities can generally then sell the appreciated assets and use the cash for their operations and have no capital gains taxes. Secondly, and perhaps more importantly, the current long-term capital gains rate is only 15%, which makes the 'keeping' rate 85%. Put another way, would you turn down a $10,000 pay raise because you didn't want to pay the IRS $1,500 in taxes? Don't let yourself get locked into thinking capital gains are a bad thing that 'cost' you. Always remember the 'keeping' rate is what matters and that taking some gains during a market rally is much better (after taxes) than potentially seeing your investment decline leaving you no gain at all.

Simple Steps to Achieving Financial Fulfillment

What could you relate to in Chapter 6?

- Are your retirement contributions going into a tax-deductible account, such as a 401(k)?

- Have you ever considered Roth accounts?

- Which one of the tax strategies mentioned might you research for use in the future?

CHAPTER 7

Protecting What You've Got

Life can be full of unexpected events, so make sure you have appropriate insurance coverage to protect your family and loved ones. Some insurance coverages are very common and even required, such as automobile and homeowners insurance, while the purpose of others are less universally understood, such as disability, life, and long-term care insurance. No matter the type, proper insurance coverage can help protect your assets or your income at various stages of life.

Automobile Insurance

It's common knowledge that if your car gets damaged in an accident, your insurance company will typically pay for the costs of repairing the vehicle and your responsibility is to pay the deductible. Deductible amounts usually range from $250 to $2,000 per covered occurrence. Generally, the lower the deductible, the higher the auto insurance rates you pay in premiums. This is because the insurance company will need to pay out more if you make a claim and have a lower deductible. For example, say you have an accident that leads to $4,000 in damages to your car. If you have collision insurance with a $500 deductible, your car insurance claim payout would be $3,500. If you instead had a $2,000 deductible, your insurance company would only pay out $2,000 on the same claim.

If you recall from Chapter 2, one reason to build a cash reserve is so that unexpected events don't feel like an emergency situation. If you have a cash reserve, you can consider raising your deductible in order to reduce your premiums each year.

According to a *Forbes Advisor* analysis of car insurance deductibles and rates, drivers who increase their deductibles can save an average of 7% to 28% each year. They go on to state that the biggest savings are typically available to drivers who make a substantial change to their deductible, such as jumping from $250 to $2,000, but you should consider what amount feels most comfortable to you. The amount you save primarily depends on your current deductible, your new deductible, and your auto insurance company.

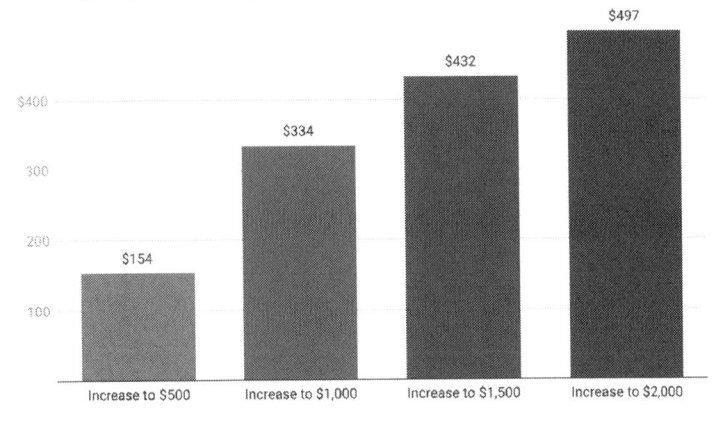

Savings by increasing a car insurance deductible from $250

Increase to $500	Increase to $1,000	Increase to $1,500	Increase to $2,000
$154	$334	$432	$497

Chart: Forbes Advisor • Source: Quadrant Information Services • Created with Datawrapper

Homeowners Insurance

Similar to auto insurance, homeowners insurance (and renters insurance) can provide essential coverage for property damage as well as injuries to people and personal liability. Changing your deductible does not have quite as dramatic of an effect on premiums as with auto coverage, but as many commercials suggest, bundling home and auto together with the same company can save you on premium costs. Also, umbrella liability insurance should be considered as you accumulate assets because it provides coverage beyond the limits of your other insurance policies. It can include additional liability coverage for injuries, damage to property, certain lawsuits, and personal liability situations.

Life Insurance

Life insurance typically provides a tax-free payout that can be used to cover bills and expenses and potentially replace the lost income from a wage earner who passes away prematurely. Many people first consider it when they experience a major life event, such as getting married, starting a family or buying a new home.

The two major types of life insurance are term and whole life. As the names imply, term policies cover only a specific number of years (the term) and whole life coverage can be for a lifetime. Term life provides a guaranteed death benefit for the term you choose, and your payments remain level for the length of the term. It is also more affordable than whole life policies and is sufficient to cover the vast majority of life insurance needs. Whole life insurance provides features beyond a simple death benefit, including the build-up of cash value, and potential access to policy loans. Of course, with these additional features comes higher premiums for the same level of insurance coverage than a comparable term policy.

Disability Insurance

Will money be available if the main wage earner or earners in a family become disabled? Disability insurance can cover this need and also has two major types: short-term and long-term. Short-term disability insurance is beneficial for situations in which an employee is injured and can return to work, whereas long-term disability helps those who will be out of work for a long time or even permanently. As you might imagine, short-term benefits begin more quickly, don't last as long, and typically cover a higher percentage of the lost income, as compared to benefits from long-term disability insurance policies.

Health Insurance

Many employers provide health insurance to their employees as a standard part of their compensation and benefits package. Self-employed individuals and those without coverage can access insurance through the federal Healthcare Marketplace. Plans available through the Marketplace can be available with a premium credit (cost savings) that is based on your annual income. Medicare health insurance coverage is generally available at age 65 for many Americans.

Long-Term Care Insurance

A long-term care insurance policy covers services that aren't covered by regular health insurance. These services can include help with bathing, dressing, or getting in and out of bed and may be provided at a nursing home or an assisted living facility. Whether long-term care insurance is the right choice depends on your situation and preferences. Long-term care insurance should be considered in your 50s to mid-60s because you most likely won't qualify for long-term care insurance once you have a debilitating condition.

Simple Steps to Achieving Financial Freedom

What could you relate to in Chapter 7?

- What is your current car insurance deductible?

- Do you know if you have enough life insurance?

- What area(s) of insurance coverage do you think you should review in the future?

CHAPTER 8

Adjusting Your Plans over Time

We know that regularly maintained vehicles are more reliable, more durable, and have a higher resale value. What about your financial plans?

Here is what to include in a checkup or an annual review of your finances:

1. Review your initial planning assumptions, and make any necessary adjustments.
2. Review any upcoming financial decisions.
3. Evaluate your overall asset allocation between stocks and bonds to determine whether rebalancing is needed to restore your original target percentages.
4. Evaluate your specific investments to determine whether they are performing in line with expectations and appropriate benchmarks. Make adjustments if necessary.
5. Evaluate your income tax return to look for deductions or ways to minimize taxes for the following year.

6. Maximize retirement account contributions where possible to reduce income taxes or consider funding Roth accounts to allow assets to receive tax-free growth.

7. Track your spending habits to determine whether you are living within your means and not negatively impacting your long-term financial plans.

8. Make sure your insurance and estate documents are up to date to reflect any changes in family dynamics and new or updated assets.

9. Coordinate your financial plan with all members of your professional team, including accountants, lawyers, and insurance providers, as necessary.

10. Communicate your plans to family members or others who may be involved at some point to ensure your intentions are known.

Your personal situation deserves specific planning and evaluation. Therefore, this is not a comprehensive list that fits every need. But as you can see, there is a lot to evaluate on a regular basis to keep up with your financial plans to ensure you reach your goals!

If a list of ten items to review seems overwhelming, just focus on these two things:

1. **Save more** – If you are working, try to put 1% or 2% more of your income into savings or a retirement account. The easiest way to save on a regular basis is if you don't have to think about it or you don't see it happen. Also, do your best to maintain an emergency fund because you never know when your car may need a costly repair or an appliance in your home will need to be replaced.

2. **Spend less** - Most everyday items have high, medium, and low-cost alternatives. Be practical most of the time, and treat yourself once in a while.

A little bit of effort can go a long way in helping yourself in the future. (I'm a big fan of future me!) It can also help to think about where you want to be or what you want to accomplish by this time next year. So rather than cleaning up a bad habit or promising yourself you'll start a good one, lay out a plan and make it happen! You'll be on your way to better financial shape if you can live within your means.

Important Age Milestones in Retirement and Why Your Half Birthday Really Does Matter

59½? 70½? 73? How does the IRS come up with these?

If you ask several young children how old they are, I'll bet at least one of them will say their age plus a half: "I'm five and a half!" They say it with pride, so you don't forget it! Once you get past age 21 there is a lull in significant birthday milestones. As you'll see, half birthdays do come into play as you get older and closer to retirement.

Age 50: Eligible for IRA catch-up provisions. In 2023, you can put an extra $1,000 a year into an IRA or Roth IRA if otherwise eligible ($7,500 total) and an additional $7,500 into a 401(k) plan ($30,000 total). Also, be on the look-out for AARP mailings and discounts to start!

Age 55: Possibly take penalty-free 401(k) withdrawals. The 10% early withdrawal penalty is lifted in cases where you leave a job after 55 and the 401(k) was from your most recent employer. But just because you can avoid a penalty doesn't mean this is necessarily a good idea for everyone. Also, you can contribute more to a Health Savings Account (HSA) once you get to this milestone.

Age 59 ½: No more 10% early withdrawal penalty for IRAs and 401(k)s. Withdrawals are still taxed as income, but the extra penalty goes away. Again, you should seek advice to determine whether this makes sense for you. Roth IRA contributions also reach one of their two flag posts that make withdrawals of contributions tax-free (the other is the account being open for 5 years). Be careful here because a separate "5-year rule" applies to each Roth IRA conversion you may have done.

Age 60: Get big discounts. Take advantage of "senior" pricing at shops, restaurants, and entertainment!

Age 62: First eligibility for Social Security. Drawing early at age 62 means you'll receive reduced benefits. If you continue to work past this age, you probably want to delay benefits because they could be reduced due to a wage limit. This goes away at full retirement age (see 66–67).

Age 65: Eligible for Medicare coverage. At this age, Medicare becomes the primary medical insurance for many people.

Age 66 – 67: Reach Social Security's "Full Retirement Age." Caps on what you can earn from a job are removed.

Age 70: Receive maximum Social Security benefits. The Delayed Retirement Credit is an increase of about 8% per year in earnings. If you waited this long to draw, your monthly benefit will be much larger than your age 62 amount would have been. However, you'll need to stick around for several more years to end up receiving more benefits than if you drew early.

Age 70½: Qualified Charitable Distributions (QCDs). Each individual can distribute up to $100,000 per year directly from their IRA custodian to a qualified public 501(c)(3) charity. Normally IRA withdrawals are taxable, so this helps reduce IRA balances used for future RMD calculations. After age 73, QCDs are even more effective because they satisfy your RMD and lower your Adjusted Gross Income (separate from using charitable gifts for itemized deductions). This may save you money on Medicare premiums and lower the taxable amount of your Social Security. There is no lower dollar limit, so even if you typically gift $1,000 or less, it all helps!

Age 73: Required Minimum Distributions must begin from most retirement accounts. The pre-tax deferral and compounding party that may have begun more than 50 years ago, when you first started working and saving, begins to wind down as you start to draw from retirement accounts.

Maybe now you can look forward to your next milestone birthday!

Simple Steps to Achieving Financial Fulfillment

What could you relate to in Chapter 8?

- What parts of your financial plan do you review most often?

- What age milestone will you reach next and how can you prepare?

CHAPTER 9

Passing on What You Have and What You Have Learned

What do you want your legacy to be? Along with your value system, family traditions, and great genetics, you will undoubtedly leave a financial legacy to the next generation. As you move through life, it may become important to you to pass on your frugalness and investment savvy, or even share some mistakes you have made in order to show how they can be avoided. Organizing your finances for your heirs can take a big burden off of your mind and an even bigger one off of their plates with some simple planning and communication. You can leave your money and values with purposeful intention, not just a list of who gets what.

Charitable Giving

If you have accumulated a significant net worth over your lifetime and are unlikely to spend it all, you may want to consider some form of gifting. You may also benefit through the form of federal tax deductions, capital gains avoidance, and reduced inheritance taxes. This is not intended to be a comprehensive list, but it is evidence that not all gifting or estate reduction strategies need to be complicated.

Gift Appreciated Investments

As you plan your charitable gifting for the year, don't forget that you can avoid the tax on appreciated securities by gifting them instead of selling them. You also may get to take a charitable deduction for the gift, saving you money in two ways! More details on this in the Donor-Advised Fund section below.

Donor-Advised Funds (DAFs)

Most large financial institutions like Schwab, Vanguard, Fidelity, etc. offer these accounts which are like a charitable savings or investing vehicle. You simply make a gift to the account (usually a $5,000 -$10,000 minimum) and it should qualify for an immediate tax deduction in the year of the gift. The funds are invested in a way you select, and as often as you want you can distribute money in the fund to the charities of your choice. By involving your kids or grandkids in the process of giving, these methods can also be a great way to encourage philanthropy in future generations.

According to the National Philanthropic Trust, these accounts were created way back in the 1930s and were not officially recognized in the tax code until the 2006 Pension Protection Act. Donor-Advised Funds can receive a variety of assets including cash, stocks, real estate, and life insurance proceeds. The DAF itself can even be the beneficiary of an IRA or trust. Donor-Advised Funds can also be very useful if the charity you want to benefit is small and doesn't have the means to accept something like a gift of stock. The stock could be gifted into the DAF followed by a grant of cash made to the charity. Also, a single transfer to an account can be split among multiple 501(c)(3) organizations.

Another benefit is that these accounts can be a great tool for someone expecting a big spike in income. The donor can make an off-setting charitable donation (for an income tax deduction) to the DAF in the year it is most effective and still have time to figure out which charities to support. This could be useful in the case of a business sale, stock option exercise, or a big bonus.

There can be a few negatives of DAFs, including large account minimums, administrative fees, irrevocable contributions, and the fact that the charity may not get all of the money right away.

Family Gifting Strategies

While many popular gifting strategies involve charities, gifting to family members can be equally rewarding. Here are a few easy approaches that can reduce or avoid taxes and are also effective wealth-transfer techniques.

Cash

Perhaps the most often practiced method, you can simply give cash, write a check, or Venmo your favorite person or grandchild. In 2023, you can gift up to $17,000 (called the annual exclusion) to an unlimited number of individuals without reporting or tax filing requirements. If you are married, you can take advantage of gift splitting, which allows for you and your spouse to gift up to $34,000 to any individual. If you give more than $17,000 in a year to any one person, you need to file a gift tax return. That doesn't mean you have to pay a gift tax, it just means you need to file IRS Form 709 to disclose the gift. Gifts between spouses and to charity are unlimited, and the recipient of a gift generally pays no tax either.

Pay College Tuition or Medical Bills Directly

There are two exceptions to the annual gifting limit. If you pay medical expenses or college tuition directly, the $17,000 limit does not apply.

Start a Roth IRA

If you are starting small with gifting to a teenage grandchild, this may be a good fit. For example, if your grandson earned $1,000 mowing lawns and would otherwise qualify, he could put $1,000 into a Roth IRA. If he saved half of what he made or $500, you could gift a matching contribution of the other half to allow him to put the full $1,000 into the account. This could be a great way to encourage saving and investing at an early age.

Gift Appreciated Assets to Lower Income Tax Brackets

You can gift stocks or other securities to someone else who will pay less tax than you upon an investment sale. Just beware of the 'Kiddie Tax,' which is levied on unearned income (interest, dividends, and capital gains) earned by children under the age of 19 and college students under 24. The first $1,250 is offset by the standard deduction, and the next $1,250 will be taxed at the child's tax rate. All of the child's unearned income in excess of $2,500 is taxed at the parent's tax rate.

State Income Tax Deduction for 529 Plan Contributions

Several states allow income tax deductions for these contributions subject to certain limits. You can be the donor for a 529 plan managed by your child where your grandchild is the beneficiary. So you may be able to help yourself with a state income tax deduction at the same time!

Estate Planning

Planning for the end of your life is a topic most people understandably want to avoid. However, without basic planning, there could be unpleasant outcomes. I have been asked several times by clients if they really need a will, and it is typically followed by a statement such as "I'm sure everything will be taken care of by my kids" or "My situation is pretty straightforward." So how basic does your situation have to be to NOT need a will? If you truly have no heirs and no worldly possessions, then you get a pass; otherwise you should probably have one.

If for no other reason, you need a will to name an executor (or executrix). This is the person responsible for handling your affairs after you pass on. If you do not have a will, the probate court will appoint one. Anyone with good reason can petition the court to be appointed so, in my opinion, there is no reason to leave this to chance. The executor or court appointed administrator performs many important functions, including gathering all of the assets of the estate, paying any debts or taxes owed by the deceased, and distributing the remaining property to the named beneficiaries.

If you die without a will, your state of residence will decide who gets what through what are called intestacy laws. These rules vary from state to state, and assets generally go to immediate family first, such as a spouse, parents, or children. If you are single with no children or surviving parents, then the state will decide who is the most important of your remaining relatives. In Pennsylvania, this is generally 1) siblings and their children, followed by 2) grandparents 3) uncles, aunts and their children and grandchildren and finally 4) the Commonwealth of Pennsylvania. Yes, if no one else is named in Pennsylvania, assets go to the state. That may be a crying shame if you had a best friend or favorite charity that was more deserving. It would be a good idea to check with a local attorney about the laws in your state and to see about getting this simple, important estate planning document in place.

The other primary estate planning documents everyone should have are a Durable Financial Power of Attorney (DPOA), Health Care Power of Attorney (HCPOA), and Living Will. Unlike a Last Will and Testament, these could all be used while you are living because you may not have full capacity to make your own decisions.

A **Durable Financial Power of Attorney** gives a trusted individual, called your agent, the legal authority to act on your behalf in financial matters. You can designate specific powers for the agent, and they generally include things like paying your bills, managing your real estate assets and financial accounts, and gifting assets to others including charity. Once you execute the DPOA and your agent acknowledges it in writing, it is in force. The agent is required to act in your best interests, so it is of the utmost importance that you name someone with the skillset to handle these financial tasks properly and the integrity to do so in your best interests.

A **Health Care Power of Attorney** is similar to a Financial Power of Attorney, but there are two main differences. The power is given to make medical decisions, as opposed to financial decisions. And the power is only in force when you are incapacitated and not at any other time.

The **Living Will** is used to guide the HCPOA in making health care decisions. Here you outline the treatment options you want if you are unable to make decisions or communicate those decisions. It's a way to make your wishes known in advance regarding possible end-of-life care and treatments. In your Health Care Power of Attorney, you designate whether your agent is required to follow your Living Will or simply use it as a guide. The HCPOA and the Living Will are often combined into one document called an Advanced Medical Directive. You need to plan ahead for uncertainties in life, and as your situation changes, you may need to update these documents.

Simple Steps to Achieving Financial Fulfillment

What could you relate to in Chapter 9?

- What are your thoughts on gifting to charities and/or family members? Is this something you have already witnessed or been a part of?

- What estate planning documents do you need to create or revise in the future?

Conclusion

Whew, we covered a lot! For those of you who are just getting started in your adult life, I understand that it may have been a little overwhelming, as there is a good amount of financial knowledge out there to digest. You can review each chapter and begin to connect the information to your life and financial circumstances. For others with more experience, this may have been more of a refresher. Hopefully, I introduced new ideas to consider and different viewpoints based on my years of working with clients in the financial planning industry.

My goal for this book is to reduce financial stress in your life. So, did it help? Are you a little more confident in your own financial situation and have some ideas about how you can continue to improve? I truly hope that is the case!

We are only here on this earth for a short while, so why not make a memorable impact! What can you share with others that you found to be valuable in this book? How to organize your financial records? When to recognize that you may be following the herd because of the fear of missing out? How much more you may be able to build up by starting early and making savings and investing automatic?

We all know people who have made a positive and lasting impact on our lives, such as our parents, friends, and family members. You too have an opportunity to be that encouraging and steady person for someone else, and what better way than to share your new financial knowledge and show someone else how to do the little things right, avoid big mistakes, and achieve financial fulfillment.

References

Chapter 1

Krockow, Eva M. Ph.D. (27 Sept 2018). "How Many Decisions Do We Make Each Day?". Psychology Today. Retrieved 23 Oct 2023 from *https://www.psychologytoday.com/us/blog/stretching-theory/201809/how-many-decisions-do-we-make-each-day*

Richards, Carl. "Behavior Gap". Retrieved 23 Oct 2023. Used with permission.

La Monica, Paul R. (8 Aug 2006). "The Fed Pauses, but...". CNN Money. Retrieved 23 Oct 2023 from *https://money.cnn.com/2006/08/08/news/economy/fed_rates/index.htm*

Coleman, Murray. (3 Apr 2023). "Dalbar QAIB 2023: Investors are Still Their Own Worst Enemies". Index Fund Advisors. Retrieved 23 Oct 2023 from *https://www.ifa.com/articles/dalbar_2016_qaib_investors_still_their_worst_enemy*

Chapter 3

Kelly, Dr. David. (30 Sept 2023). "Guide to the Markets". J.P. Morgan Asset Management. Retrieved 23 Oct 2023 from *https://am.jpmorgan.com/us/en/asset-management/adv/insights/market-insights/guide-to-the-markets/*

Pierce, Rod. (1 Feb 2022). "Normal Distribution". Math Is Fun. Retrieved 23 Oct 2023 from *http://www.mathsisfun.com/data/standard-normal-distribution.html*

Chapter 4

Hicks, Coryanne and Hellman, Nate. (3 Aug 2023). "Impact of When You Start Investing". US News Money. Retrieved 23 Oct 2023 from *https://money.usnews.com/investing/investing-101/articles/2018-07-23/9-charts-showing-why-you-should-invest-today*, assumes 7% growth per year.

MI Research Team. (19 Sept 2018). "The Risk-Return Trade-Off". Model Investing. Retrieved 23 Oct 2023 from *https://modelinvesting.com/articles/the-risk-return-trade-off/*

Chapter 6

Cunningham, Cathryn. (4 Jan 2021). "Start the New Year with a Look at the Roth IRA". Albuquerque Journal. Retrieved 23 Oct 2023 from *https://www.abqjournal.com/business/start-the-new-year-with-a-look-at-the-roth-ira/article_2ca7b3ad-2c2a-5d01-8aaf-3da67269beae.html*

Chapter 7

Gusner, Penny. (27 Nov 2022). "How Much Can You Save by Raising Your Car Insurance Deductible?". Forbes Advisor. Retrieved 23 Oct 2023 from *https://www.forbes.com/advisor/car-insurance/savings-by-raising-car-insurance-deductible/*

Made in the USA
Middletown, DE
15 November 2024